Dedication Page

This book is dedicated to,

THE CUSTOMER

"The only purpose of a business is to create a customer."
Charlie Munger

CONTENTS

3 Preface

5 Introduction to HatClps

7 Touchstones and Touchpoints

11 HatClp Fast Start Checklist

12 What makes you, unique? Value Proposition!

15 Sales Precursors

    15 Clarity
    22 Questions
    26 Master Sales Inquiries, BONUS
    31 Content

35 Evaluate & Re-define Your Market

38 Target Market Review

41 Target Qualifying System

43 Referrals are a Game Changer

45 Word of Mouth Strategy (WOM), peer to peer!

47 Summary

Preface

My name is William Bowser II, and I was born in September 1968 in Western Pennsylvania. Growing up in a modest household, my brother and I shared a small bedroom until our teenage years. We spent most of our childhood playing outside, as we had limited access to video games, the internet, or even much television. This upbringing instilled in me a strong work ethic and a drive to seek out opportunities where none seemed to exist. My professional journey has been transformative. I served as the CEO of Redemption Amusement Inc., a successful vending company in Pittsburgh, Pennsylvania, for 13 years. Currently, I am the CEO of BladeCo Inc., an industrial laser marking company that also provides laser-grade promotional products to businesses. My career has been a testament to the power of perseverance, innovation, and dedication. Over the years, I have distilled my experiences and insights into two previous books. "The Nine Elements of Business Success" draws on my extensive business background to offer practical advice on navigating the complexities of entrepreneurship. "VIRTUE" is a deeply personal work, inspired by my life's lessons and intended as a legacy of wisdom for my children and future generations. In "The Secret Touchstone," I aim to bridge the worlds of business acumen and personal fulfillment. This book explores the critical framework of touch points and touchstones in marketing and customer engagement, emphasizing the dynamic potential of tools like HatClps. By understanding and leveraging these concepts, businesses can create lasting connections with their audiences and drive meaningful engagement. My journey has been one of constant learning and growth, and I am excited to share these insights with you. For those who wish to connect with me or follow my journey, you can reach out to me on LinkedIn. I hope "The Secret Touchstone" serves as a valuable resource for your personal and professional development, just as my previous works have been inspired by my life's experiences and lessons. Thank you for embarking on this journey with me. Together, let us unlock the secrets to success and fulfillment.

Introduction

Hatclps are simply the best tool for your business to create a word-of-mouth marketing strategy by utilizing Automatic Customer Engagement tactics.

This strategy is delivered through a set of well-designed precursors that address those crucial moments prior to a person becoming a customer.

Automatic **C**ustomer **E**ngagement **M**arketing, ACEM provides analytical guidance for a business to refine their touch points with customers and prospects. The Hatclp is the premier touchstone for automatic customer engagement success and prospect conversion.

ACE marketing acts as a strategic partner with companies providing advanced levels of insight into your customers wants and needs.

Listed below are some **great benefits** you may experience by adding the HATCLP to your company's marketing toolbox.

1. Highly visible
2. Mobile advertisement
3. Unique
4. Affordable

5. Durable
6. Collectible
7. Awesome Fundraiser
8. Creates Awareness
9. A conversation starter
10. Generates talking points
11. Great ice breaker
12. Conversation extender
13. Reveals insights about the customer
14. LINK your website
15. Free Artwork
16. Free Shipping
17. Free Marketing Guide when you buy 300 Hatclps
18. HATCLPS are just cool!

Touchstones and Touchpoints

In the vast landscape of marketing strategies, the concept of touch points and touchstones has emerged as a critical framework for businesses aiming to engage their audience effectively. At the forefront of this movement lies HatClps, a versatile tool that transcends traditional marketing approaches, offering a dynamic blend of automatic customer engagement and prospect conversion. Let's delve into the realm of touch points and touchstones, exploring how businesses can harness the power of HatClps to elevate their marketing endeavors. Understanding Touch Points and how they represent every interaction a customer has with a business throughout their journey, from initial awareness to post-purchase engagement. These interactions serve as pivotal moments where businesses can leave a lasting impression, ultimately influencing purchasing decisions. HatClps, with its multifaceted benefits, seamlessly integrates into various touch points, amplifying brand visibility and fostering customer engagement. The Role of Touchstones, on the other hand, are key elements within the customer journey that serve as reference points for brand interactions. They encapsulate the essence of a brand, evoking emotions and memories that resonate with customers. HatClps emerges as a premier touchstone, offering a unique blend of functionality and novelty that leaves a memorable imprint on customers' minds. Unlocking the power of HatClps as more than just an accessory energizes meaningful engagement and brand advocacy. Let's dissect the various benefits that HatClps bring to the table:

1. High Visibility

With HatClps adorning hats, bags, and various accessories, businesses can enjoy heightened visibility in diverse settings, ensuring maximum exposure for their brand.

2. Mobile Advertising

Leveraging the mobility of HatClps, businesses can extend their reach far beyond traditional advertising channels, tapping into new demographics and markets.

3. Uniqueness

In a sea of marketing gimmicks, HatClps shine as a unique and eye-catching promotional tool, setting businesses apart from competitors and garnering attention effortlessly.

4. Affordability

Cost-effective yet impactful, HatClps offer businesses a budget-friendly solution to amplify their marketing efforts without compromising on quality or effectiveness.

5. Durability

Built to withstand the rigors of daily use, HatClps ensure long-term brand exposure, becoming enduring symbols of quality and reliability in customers' lives.

6. Collectability

HatClps possess inherent collectible value, enticing customers to seek out and accumulate different designs, thereby fostering brand loyalty and repeat engagement.

7. Fundraising

Beyond marketing, HatClps serve as excellent fundraising tools, enabling organizations to generate revenue while simultaneously promoting their cause or brand.

8. Awareness Creation

By sparking curiosity and intrigue, HatClps effectively raise awareness about a brand or cause, initiating conversations and driving engagement organically.

9. Conversation Starter

The unique design and versatility of HatClps make them natural conversation starters, facilitating meaningful interactions and brand advocacy among customers.

10. Generating Talking Points

Each HatClps design tells a story, providing businesses with a wealth of talking points to engage customers and build rapport effortlessly.

11. Ice Breaker

In social settings or networking events, HatClps serve as icebreakers, bridging the gap between strangers and fostering connections based on shared interests and affiliations.

12. Conversation Extender

With HatClps sparking initial conversations, businesses can seamlessly extend these interactions into deeper engagements, nurturing relationships and driving conversions.

13. **Revealing Customer Insights**

Through customer interactions with HatClps, businesses gain valuable insights into consumer preferences, behaviors, and trends, empowering them to refine their marketing strategies and offerings effectively.

14. **Cool Factor**

Let's not forget the undeniable cool factor of HatClps. As a trendy and sought-after accessory, HatClps effortlessly elevate the brand's image, attracting a diverse audience of trendsetters and influencers. Incorporating HatClps into a business's marketing arsenal promises to revolutionize their approach to customer engagement and prospect conversion.

Now, let's outline a fast start checklist to guide you in leveraging HatClps effectively.

HatClps Fast Start Checklist

1. Define Objectives

Clearly outline the marketing objectives and target audience demographics to align HatClps initiatives with overarching business goals.

2. Select Designs

Choose HatClps designs that resonate with the brand's identity and messaging, ensuring consistency across all touch points.

3. Strategic Placement

Identify strategic locations and touch points to distribute HatClps, maximizing visibility and engagement opportunities.

4. Employee Training

Educate staff members on the benefits and usage of HatClps to empower them as brand ambassadors and advocates.

5. Integration with Marketing Channels

Seamlessly integrate HatClps into existing marketing channels, such as social media, events, and promotions, to amplify reach and impact.

6. Track and Measure

Implement tracking mechanisms to monitor the effectiveness of HatClps initiatives, gathering insights to refine strategies and optimize results.

7. **Engage Customers**

Encourage customer participation and feedback through interactive campaigns and contests centered around HatClps, fostering a sense of community and brand loyalty. By following this comprehensive checklist, businesses can harness the full potential of HatClps as a transformative tool for sales and marketing touch points, driving meaningful customer engagement and propelling brand growth in the digital age. HatClps stand as the epitome of innovation and effectiveness in the realm of automatic customer engagement and prospect conversion. As businesses navigate the ever-evolving landscape of marketing, HatClps emerge as indispensable allies, guiding them towards unparalleled success and enduring customer relationships.

What Makes You Unique? Value Proposition!

The single biggest problem with communication is the assumption……………………...that it has taken place.

By asking appropriate, well-planned questions during a customer interview or a sales-call will give you great insights and understanding about that person. Your primary competitor is not another company or brand but rather it is ALL THE NOISE and distraction that your customer faces every day. You must cut through that NOISE and **create a relevant message that speaks to their wants.**

Let's create a comprehensive framework for crafting a compelling business value proposition. We'll start with the basics and gradually delve into more specialized aspects. Here's a step-by-step process:

Step 1: Understanding Your Audience

1. Who are your target customers?

2. What are their needs, desires, and pain points?

3. How does your product or service address these needs better than competitors?

Step 2: Analyzing Your Offering

1. What are the key features and benefits of your product or service?

2. How does it solve specific problems or fulfill specific desires?

3. What unique advantages does it offer over alternatives?

Step 3: Competitive Analysis

1. Who are your main competitors?

2. What are their value propositions?

3. How does your offering differentiate from theirs?

Step 4: Defining Your Value Proposition

1. What is the core benefit or solution your offering provides?

2. What makes it unique and desirable to your target audience?

3. How can you communicate this succinctly and effectively?

Step 5: <u>Crafting the Value Proposition Statement</u>

1. Summarize the key benefit of your product or service.

2. Describe who it's for and why they should care.

3. Highlight the unique value or advantage it offers.

Step 6: <u>Refining and Testing</u>

1. Get feedback from potential customers and stakeholders.

2. Iterate based on feedback to clarify and strengthen the value proposition.

3. Test different versions to see which resonates most with your audience.

Step 7: Implementing and Monitoring

1. Incorporate the value proposition into your marketing materials and messaging.

2. Track metrics such as customer engagement, conversion rates, and sales to assess its effectiveness.

3. Continuously refine and adapt based on performance and market changes.

Step 8: Scaling and Optimization

1. As your business grows, ensure the value proposition remains relevant and compelling.

2. Explore opportunities to expand or refine your offering based on evolving customer needs.

3. Continuously seek ways to optimize and improve the value proposition for maximum impact. By following these steps and asking yourself these guiding questions, you can systematically develop a strong and effective value proposition that resonates with your target audience and sets your business apart from competitors.

Sales Precursors

- ## Clarity, precursor #1

Steve Woodruff's 5 elements of clarity - the what, for whom, the why, the how, and the where - are a useful framework for businesses to communicate their value proposition clearly to potential customers.

- The "what" refers to the product or service being offered. It's essential that businesses clearly communicate what they're selling and what benefits it provides.

- The "for whom" refers to the target market or customer that the product or service is intended for. It's important for businesses to understand who their ideal customer is and tailor their messaging accordingly.

- The "why" refers to the problem or need that the product or service solves. It's essential for businesses to clearly communicate the value that their product or service provides and how it addresses the customer's needs.
- The "how" refers to the method or process that the business uses to deliver the product or service. This includes the features and benefits, pricing, and any guarantees or warranties offered.
- The "where" refers to the channels or platforms where the business will market and sell the product or service.

By addressing all five elements of clarity, businesses can create a clear and compelling message that resonates with their target market and effectively communicates the value of their product or service. This can be used in a variety of marketing channels, such as website, social media, email campaigns, and advertising.

Additionally, it's also important to ensure that the message is consistent across all marketing channels to avoid confusion and ensure a clear understanding of the value proposition.

Clarity is essential for any business that wants to be successful in today's competitive market. It is the foundation of good communication, and it allows businesses to effectively communicate their value proposition to potential customers. When a business is clear about what it offers, who it is for, why it is needed, how it is delivered, and where it can be found, it makes it easy for potential customers to understand the value of the product or service and make informed decisions.

But clarity is not only important for the customer, but it also benefits the business. When a business is **clear** about its **value proposition**, it helps to **define its target market**, which in turn helps to identify the most **effective marketing** channels and messaging. A clear message also helps to increase brand awareness and **build trust** with customers.

In addition, clarity can help to **streamline the sales process**. When a business is clear about its value proposition, it's **easier to** identify the most **qualified leads** and close more deals. It also helps to reduce the need for price negotiation, as the customer understands the value of the product or service.

Clarity also helps to **improve the customer experience**. When a customer understands the value of a product or service, they are more likely to be satisfied with their purchase and **become loyal customers**. This, in turn, can lead to increased repeat business and positive word-of-mouth referrals.

In a nutshell, clarity is an essential ingredient for any business that wants to be successful. By being clear about its value proposition, a business can attract the right customers, close more deals, improve the customer experience and ultimately increase its revenue. It's time to embrace clarity and let it work wonders for your business.

Let's dive deeper into each step with actionable tactics:

1. Define Your Target Market: - Conduct thorough market research to understand the demographics, preferences, and behaviors of your target audience. - Create buyer personas to represent different segments of your target market, including their goals, challenges, and purchasing motivations. - Use tools like Google Analytics, social media insights, and customer surveys to gather data and refine your understanding of your audience. - Regularly update your buyer personas as you gather more information and insights from customer interactions and market trends.

2. Craft a Compelling Value Proposition: - Identify the unique benefits and features of your product or service that set it apart from competitors. - Clearly communicate how your offering solves specific problems or meets specific needs of your target audience. - Use language that resonates with your audience's emotions and aspirations, focusing on the outcomes they desire. - Test different value propositions with your target market to determine which resonates most effectively. - Continuously refine and evolve your value proposition based on customer feedback and market dynamics.

3. Develop Clear Messaging: - Use simple, straightforward language that is easy for your target audience to understand. - Clearly communicate the key benefits of your product or service without using unnecessary jargon. - Structure your messaging to address common pain points or objections your audience may have. - Use storytelling techniques to make your messaging more engaging and memorable. - Test your messaging across different channels and mediums to ensure consistency and effectiveness.

4. Create Visual Content: - Invest in professional graphic design to create visually appealing images and graphics that align with your brand identity. - Use high-quality photographs and videos to showcase your product or service in action. - Incorporate infographics and visualizations to simplify complex information and make it easier for your audience to understand. - Optimize visual content for mobile devices to ensure a seamless user experience across all platforms. - Track engagement metrics for visual content to identify which types resonate most with your audience.

5. Design User-Friendly Interfaces: - Conduct usability testing to identify any friction points or usability issues with your website or app. - **Simplify** navigation menus and use clear labels to help users find what they're looking for quickly. - **Minimize the number of steps** required to complete common tasks, such as making a purchase or filling out a form. - **Provide helpful tooltips and guidance** throughout the user journey to assist users who may be unfamiliar with your interface. - Regularly review and update your interface design based on user feedback and analytics data.

6. Implement a Content Calendar: - Plan your content strategy around key events, holidays, and industry trends to stay relevant and timely. - Use a content calendar tool to schedule and organize your content across different channels and platforms. - Allocate resources and assign responsibilities to ensure consistent execution of your content plan. - Monitor performance metrics for each piece of content to identify top-performing topics and formats. - Adjust your content calendar based on performance data and feedback to optimize results over time.

7. Provide Clear Calls to Action (CTAs): - Use action-oriented language that prompts users to take specific steps, such as "Shop Now" or "Request a Quote." - Place CTAs prominently on your website and in your marketing materials to ensure they are easily visible. - Use contrasting colors and compelling design elements to draw attention to your CTAs. - Test different wording and placement options to determine which CTAs drive the highest conversion rates. - Continuously optimize and iterate on your CTAs based on performance data and user feedback.

8. Test and Iterate: - Conduct A/B tests on different messaging, visuals, and CTAs to identify what resonates most with your audience. - Test variations of landing pages, email subject lines, and ad copy to determine which elements drive the best results. - Use multivariate testing to analyze the impact of multiple changes simultaneously. - Monitor performance metrics in real-time and make adjustments as needed to optimize campaign performance. - Document and share insights from testing experiments with your team to inform future decision-making.

9. Train Your Team: - Provide ongoing training and resources to help your team members understand the importance of clear communication. - Develop guidelines and best practices for writing and designing content that aligns with your brand voice and messaging. - Conduct regular workshops and seminars to reinforce key communication principles and techniques. - Encourage open communication and feedback within your team to foster a culture of continuous improvement. - Recognize and reward team members who consistently demonstrate excellence in communication.

10. Monitor Performance Metrics: - Set up tracking mechanisms to monitor key performance indicators (KPIs) such as website traffic, conversion rates, and engagement metrics. - Use analytics tools to gain insights into user behavior and preferences, such as heatmaps and session recordings. - Analyze trends and patterns in your data to identify areas for improvement and opportunities for growth. - Create customized reports and dashboards to track progress towards your communication goals. - Regularly review and analyze performance metrics to inform strategic decision-making and resource allocation.

11. Seek Customer Feedback: - Implement feedback mechanisms such as surveys, feedback forms, and customer reviews to gather insights from your audience. - Actively listen to customer feedback and respond promptly to address any concerns or issues raised. - Analyze feedback data to identify recurring themes and areas for improvement in your communication strategy. - Use feedback to guide iterative improvements to your messaging, content, and user experience. - Engage with customers directly through social media, forums, and community platforms to build relationships and gather insights.

12. Stay Updated: - Stay informed about industry trends, changes in consumer behavior, and emerging technologies that may impact your communication strategy. - Monitor competitors and industry leaders to identify new opportunities and best practices. - Attend conferences, webinars, and networking events to stay connected with industry peers and thought leaders. - Subscribe to relevant publications, blogs, and newsletters to stay up to date on the latest developments in your field. - Incorporate insights from industry experts and thought leaders into your communication strategy to stay ahead of the curve.

13. Continuously Improve: - Foster a culture of experimentation and innovation within your organization to encourage new ideas and approaches. - Encourage cross-functional collaboration and knowledge sharing to leverage diverse perspectives and expertise. - Regularly review and evaluate your communication strategy to identify areas for improvement and optimization. - Set measurable goals and benchmarks to track progress and success over time. - Celebrate successes and milestones along the way to maintain momentum and motivation for continuous improvement.

Questions, precursor #2

To truly connect with your customers and understand their needs, you must tap into their hopes, dreams, desires, and problems. By understanding what drives them to make a purchase, you can build a relationship of trust and intimacy with them. To do this it's crucial to develop a framework for asking the right questions at the right time.

Asking questions is the first step in understanding your customers' thought process. When formulated correctly, questions can open the door for customers to share information they may not have otherwise. It's essential to **develop a series of questions prior to any sales visit**, specifically designed to uncover the customer's deepest emotions surrounding their business problems. This is often referred to as "finding the hurt," and your job is to ease that pain.

By uncovering what is causing your customer discomfort and stress, you will have a clear understanding of what they need and how you can provide relief. This is your opportunity to present well-crafted questions that will ultimately lead your customer to see the value you can bring to their business. By taking this approach, you can create a deeper level of connection with your customer and build a stronger, more successful business.

For you to master and amplify the WOM strategy in your automatic customer engagement system, a series of questions must be answered to bring a clear vison of the path to your success.

Question 1: What are you providing for the market, what problem are you solving?

Question 2: Whom are you providing it for and Why do they need it?

Question 3: Where is all of this going to take place? Geographically and communicatively.

Question 4: How? What is your SUPERPOWER? How are you unique?

Sales and marketing experts often use a variety of questions to understand customer needs, motivations, and preferences. Here are types of questions commonly used during customer interviews and sales calls to draw out insights about buying motivations:

1. **Open-Ended Questions:** - Encourage customers to share detailed information. - Example: "Can you tell me more about your experience with [product/service]?"

2. **Probing Questions:** - Delve deeper into specific areas of interest. - Example: "What challenges are you currently facing in your [industry/process]?"

3. **Clarifying Questions:** - Seek further explanation to ensure a clear understanding. - Example: "Could you elaborate on how [specific aspect] impacts your decision-making?"

4. **Problem-Agitate-Solution Questions:** - Identify issues, emphasize their importance, and propose solutions. - Example: "Have you noticed any inefficiencies in your current [process]? How has that affected your team's productivity? We have a solution that addresses these challenges."

5. **Leading Questions:** - Guide the customer toward a particular perspective. - Example: "Would having a more streamlined [product/service] significantly impact your team's efficiency?"

6. **Value-Based Questions:**- Explore the value that the customer places on specific features or benefits. - Example: "How would improved [feature] positively affect your overall business goals?"

7. **Future-Oriented Questions:** - Encourage customers to envision positive outcomes. - Example: "Can you imagine how [product/service] might contribute to your long-term success?"

8. **Budget and Affordability Questions:** - Assess the customer's financial considerations. - Example: "What budget range are you working with for this particular solution?"

9. **Timeline Questions:** - Explore the customer's timeframe for making a decision. - Example: "When do you plan on implementing a solution for [specific need]?"

10. **Competitor Comparison Questions:** - Understand the customer's perception of your competitors. - Example: "How do you currently compare our [product/service] with those offered by our competitors?" Remember that the key is to actively listen to the customer's responses and tailor subsequent questions based on the information provided. This approach helps build a deeper understanding of the customer's needs and motivations, ultimately facilitating a more effective sales process.

Notes: Questions that get them to tell you stories:

Their origin story?

Their success stories?

Their failures stories?

Master Sales Inquiries & Unveil Customer Stories

The Power of Origin Stories

In the world of sales, understanding the origin story of your potential customers is akin to unlocking a treasure trove of invaluable insights. The journey from inception to the present provides a nuanced understanding of their needs, aspirations, and the driving forces behind their decision-making. When customers share their origin stories, they reveal the very essence of their business or personal journey and the importance of building rapport becomes evident. Learning about a customer's origin fosters a sense of connection. It allows the salesperson to align their approach with the customer's values and history and provides opportunity to develop tailored solutions: By grasping the challenges faced during the early stages, a salesperson can tailor their pitch to present solutions that resonate with the customer's past struggles and aspirations. - Establishing Trust: Sharing personal or business history requires a level of trust. Active listening during this phase sets the foundation for a strong, trustworthy relationship.

The Tapestry of Success

Every customer has a unique tapestry woven with threads of success. Unraveling these threads through thoughtful questions not only showcases the customer's achievements but also highlights their priorities and what they value most in a partnership. Success stories are windows into the customer's aspirations and provide the salesperson with crucial information to align their offerings with the customer's goals.

Understanding priorities and success stories often highlight the milestones that matter most to the customer. This knowledge helps the salesperson emphasize features or benefits that align with these priorities and creates positive associations. **Associating your product or service with the customer's successes creates a positive mindset.** It positions your offering as a catalyst for continued achievement and identifies patterns. Successes can reveal patterns in the customer's decision-making and recognizing these patterns allows the salesperson to predict future needs and preferences.

Embracing Failure

A Crucible for Growth* Delving into a customer's bad experiences and failures is not about dwelling on negativity but rather about understanding the lessons learned and the resilience gained. Mistakes are often steppingstones to success, and exploring these aspects of a customer's journey provides profound insights into their resilience, adaptability, and the specific pain points they aim to address.

Importance: Identifying Pain Points: Failures often pinpoint areas where the customer faced challenges. Addressing these pain points becomes a focal point for the salesperson to offer tailored solutions.

Showcasing Empathy: Acknowledging failures with empathy builds a genuine connection. Customers appreciate a salesperson who understands their struggles and is committed to helping them overcome obstacles.

Crafting Solutions: Understanding past failures allows the salesperson to craft solutions that not only meet current needs but also provide safeguards against repeating past mistakes.

Crafting the Symphony of Questions and Mastering the art of asking questions in sales is like conducting a symphony. Each note, each question, plays a unique role in unveiling the customer's story. Active listening becomes the conductor's baton, revealing insights that guide the salesperson to compose their next well-thought-out question. By navigating through the origin, successes, and failures of the customer's journey, a salesperson not only builds a robust understanding of the customer's buying motivations but also forges a meaningful and lasting partnership.

The Power of Origin Stories Cont'd

In the ever-evolving landscape of sales and marketing, the significance of understanding the origin stories of customers cannot be overstated. It serves as the cornerstone for building meaningful connections, crafting tailored solutions, and ultimately driving successful outcomes. While technological advancements and data analytics have undoubtedly enhanced the sales process, it is the art of active listening and gathering insights directly from customers that remains paramount in today's competitive environment.

Active Listening

Active listening is not merely the act of hearing words; it is a dynamic process that involves fully engaging with the speaker and comprehending the underlying messages. Research conducted by Harvard Business Review has consistently highlighted active listening as a foundational skill for effective communication, particularly in sales interactions. Sales professionals who master this skill demonstrate genuine interest in their customers' stories, fostering trust and rapport that are essential for long-term relationships. In the context of origin stories, active listening enables sales professionals to glean valuable insights into the journey, challenges, and triumphs of their customers. By attentively listening to the nuances of their narratives, sales professionals can identify key turning points, motivations, and aspirations that shape the customer's decision-making process. This deep understanding forms the basis for personalized recommendations and solutions that resonate with the customer's unique circumstances.

Gathering Customer Insights

Customer insights are the lifeblood of effective sales strategies, providing invaluable guidance for decision-making and strategy formulation. Influential thought leaders in marketing, such as Simon Sinek, emphasize the importance of understanding the "why" behind customer behavior. By exploring the origin stories of customers, sales professionals gain access to a wealth of insights that illuminate the underlying motivations, values, and preferences driving their actions. Practical Application of Data: Incorporating the principles of active listening and gathering customer insights into sales practices requires a multifaceted approach that blends old-school methods with the latest technology.

1. **Old School Methods:** Traditional techniques such as face-to-face meetings, phone calls, and personalized emails remain indispensable tools for gathering customer insights. During these interactions, sales professionals have the opportunity to engage in meaningful conversations, ask probing questions, and actively listen to the customer's responses. Taking diligent notes and observing non-verbal cues further enhance the understanding of the customer's origin story, allowing for the identification of pain points and areas of opportunity.

2. **Latest Technology:** In the digital age, sales professionals have access to a myriad of technological tools that streamline the process of gathering customer insights. Customer Relationship Management (CRM) software serves as a centralized repository for storing and analyzing customer data, facilitating a comprehensive view of the customer's journey. Advanced analytics tools leverage machine learning algorithms to uncover patterns and trends in customer behavior, enabling sales professionals to anticipate needs and deliver personalized experiences. Social media platforms such as LinkedIn provide a wealth of information about a prospect's professional background, interests, and connections, offering valuable context for initiating conversations and building rapport.

With a deep understanding of their customers' journeys, challenges, and aspirations, sales professionals can forge authentic connections, tailor solutions that address specific needs, and ultimately drive positive outcomes for both their customers and their businesses. In an era characterized by rapid technological advancement and shifting consumer preferences, the ability to harness the human element of sales remains a timeless and indispensable skill.

Content, precursor #3

Get **More Customers by Marketing Less** In the realm of content marketing, an intriguing concept is to attract more customers by marketing less. This approach hinges on the principles of informing, entertaining, and compelling action through **strategic content creation**. A successful content marketing strategy should focus on developing content as an asset, not an expense, to cultivate a loyal audience within a specific niche. This audience-building strategy is foundational to ensuring long-term business growth and success.

Developing a Content Marketing Strategy is a key aspect of managing content marketing is recognizing that content should function as an asset. Unlike traditional advertising, which is often viewed as an expense with a fleeting impact, content marketing involves creating valuable content that continues to attract and engage customers over time. This perspective shift is crucial; instead of seeing content creation as a cost center, it should be regarded as a long-term investment that can yield substantial returns. To achieve this, focus on a specific niche and build a loyal audience within that niche. This involves understanding your target audience's needs, interests, and pain points, and then consistently delivering content that addresses these areas. A well-defined niche allows you to tailor your messaging more precisely, making it more relevant and compelling to your audience.

The Value of a Newsletter is one of the most effective content vehicles for building a loyal audience is a newsletter. Unlike social media, where algorithms often limit the visibility of your content, a newsletter ensures that your message reaches your audience directly. It serves as a reliable touchpoint with your subscribers, allowing you to deliver valuable information consistently. The value of a newsletter lies in its ability to provide meaningful content that resonates with your audience. This could include industry insights, tips, exclusive offers, or thought leadership pieces. The key is to focus on delivering value rather than overtly promoting your products or services. When your audience perceives your newsletter as a valuable resource, they are more likely to remain engaged and loyal.

Building Value Through Content, the primary objective of content marketing is to get customers to pay attention to you through value messaging. This means creating content that is informative, entertaining, and actionable. Informative content educates your audience about topics relevant to their interests or industry. Entertaining content engages them emotionally, making your brand more relatable and memorable. Compelling content drives action, encouraging your audience to take the next step, whether it's signing up for a newsletter, downloading a resource, or making a purchase. Once you establish a loyal audience through valuable content, there will be appropriate times to mention your products and services. However, these mentions should be subtle and contextually relevant, ensuring they enhance rather than disrupt the user experience. The goal is to integrate your offerings naturally within the content flow, making them an organic extension of the value you provide.

Audience Building as a Long-Term Asset Building an opted-in audience is a strategic asset that continues to generate value over time. Unlike paid advertisements, which stop yielding results once the budget is exhausted, an engaged audience remains a source of ongoing business opportunities. This audience can be nurtured and leveraged to promote new products, gather feedback, and even advocate for your brand. To build and maintain this audience, it is essential to deliver consistent value through your content. This involves regular communication and engagement, ensuring that your audience feels valued and heard. By focusing on audience building, you create a self-sustaining ecosystem that supports your business growth.

Content Vehicles in marketing content vehicles such as newsletters and social media play distinct roles in your marketing approach. A well-crafted newsletter provides concrete value, ensuring direct communication with your audience. In contrast, social media, often described as rented land, offers limited visibility due to platform algorithms. Typically, less than one percent of your followers see your content organically on social media. Therefore, while social media can be a useful tool for initial audience engagement and amplification, it should not be the sole focus of your content strategy.

Return on Objective, in content marketing, a critical concept is "Return on Objective" (ROO). This involves identifying and tracking specific objectives for your content efforts. Start by listing your communications with customers, such as newsletters, blog posts, social media updates, and webinars.

Next, outline the objectives for each communication type. Objectives could include increasing brand awareness, generating leads, driving website traffic, or enhancing customer loyalty. By setting clear objectives, you can measure the effectiveness of your content marketing efforts. This approach allows you to make data-driven decisions, optimizing your strategy based on what works best for your audience.

Focused Approach Over Volume When it comes to content marketing, more is not necessarily better. A focused approach, tailored to your audience's preferences and needs, is more effective than producing a high volume of content with little strategic direction. Quality trumps quantity, ensuring that each piece of content delivers maximum value. Building an audience-first strategy is a reliable and high-quality approach. This means prioritizing the needs and interests of your audience in your content planning. By doing so, you build value outside of your products and services, establishing your brand as a trusted resource and thought leader in your niche.

The concept of getting more customers by marketing less is rooted in the principles of value-driven content marketing. By treating content as an asset, focusing on a specific niche, and building a loyal audience, you create a sustainable marketing strategy that continues to yield returns over time. A well-crafted newsletter, regular value-driven communication, and a focused approach are key components of this strategy. By prioritizing quality and audience engagement, you establish a strong foundation for long-term business success.

Evaluate, Re-define your target market?

Take charge of your customer engagement! Many folks overlook opportunities because they are busy with other business. We can help bridge that gap. We see ourselves as strategic partners in your success. Our method for displaying your company logo and practical strategies will help you connect with customers in a powerful way. The following information will put you on the fast track to success by fostering relationships with key customers. It shows that traditional marketing has its place but it's not always best in today's world. Inside, you'll find statistics and strategies that have been proven to work. We are glad you're working with us to enhance your customer engagement.

Most businesses, from 50 to 90%, acquire new customers through word-of-mouth marketing by means of customer engagement, making it the most effective marketing strategy to gain new customers.

Trust makes people 4 times more likely to try something if they get a recommendation from someone they know, it's **the trust factor**. Trust is the key element that drives customer engagement and word of mouth marketing, making it the most effective way to gain new customers.

Customers tend to rely heavily on emotional buying habits, with most decisions being swayed by emotions in some form or another. Therefore, word of mouth marketing through building trust and customer engagement, is the most effective way to acquire new customers, with **50 to 90% of all business coming from referrals.** This is because people are 4 times more likely to try something if they get a recommendation from someone they know. People tend to remember how a brand made them feel, rather than what it said, and relationships and emotions play a significant role in decision-making. In contrast, print ads and social media are only responsible for 5 to 10% of business, despite their prevalence. This is because they don't provide the same emotional connection as word-of-mouth marketing and personal recommendations.

FACT: Less than 1% of all businesses have a strategy to utilize this approach.

One reason is a lack of understanding of the power and potential of word-of-mouth marketing. Many businesses may not realize the impact that building trust and fostering relationships with customers can have on their bottom line.

Another barrier is a lack of resources or knowledge on how to effectively execute a word-of-mouth marketing strategy. Businesses may not have the time, staff, or expertise to effectively implement and manage such a strategy.

A target market is a crucial aspect of any business strategy. It's a specific group of consumers that a company has identified as the most likely to benefit from its products, services, and marketing activities. Identifying and understanding your target market is essential for creating effective marketing campaigns and reaching the right people with your message. The term "target audience" is even more specific, referring to the group of consumers that a company's advertising is specifically designed to reach. Having a clear understanding of both your target market and target audience is key to creating a successful marketing strategy that drives results. In short, identifying a target market and target audience is the first step towards creating a successful marketing strategy that will reach the right people, with the right message at the right time.

Exercise for you:

EXAMPLE: Target market is motorcycle riders; a Target audience could be motorcycle advocacy groups and even further narrowing the band could be targeting geographical areas like states.

List your Target market, target audiences and identify niches with specific needs.

This will help you to be more focused on your customers and allow marketing efforts to be more effective. This method is more efficient, delivering the right message to the same group of people, rather than the scattergun approach.

Well known ways to segment your target audiences include:

1. Demographics - Breakdown by and combination of: age, gender, income, education, ethnicity, marital   status,

household (or business) size, length of residence, type of residence or even profession/occupation.

2. Psychographic - This refers to 'personality and emotions' based on behavior, linked to purchase choices including attitudes, lifestyle, hobbies, risk aversion, personality and leadership traits magazines read, and favorite TV shows. While demographics explain 'who' your buyer is, psychographics inform you 'why' your customer buys.

There are a few different ways you can gather data to help form psychographics profiles for your typical customers. Remember people don't want what you sell... They want their problems solved. For example, the man shopping for a drill bit ideally wants a hole in something. The hole may be needed to install a hook to hang a picture of a loved one. So, does he really desire a drill bit? Identifying buying motivations are the key, they lead to providing customers with better solutions and ultimately HAPPINESS. Perform customer interviews and surveys. Also ask for testimonials from your best customers and prompt them for product review (online preferably).

Target market review

Who? Why? How can you solve their problems?

Target audience review? Segment within the market?

How... method of communication?

List your best customers in terms of revenue.

1.

2.

3.

4.

5.

What makes them ideal customers for you? Other than profits.

Why do you think they do business with you?

Who would pay for my products and or services?

Who is already paying for It?

Why are they paying for it?

Who is buying it from somebody else?

Why?

Are you making assumptions about your targets based on knowledge and experience?

Get feedback from your best customers, the "promoters".

Ask them, why did you buy it from me?

Ask them, how would you describe your interaction with my company?

1. Satisfied? 2. Happy? Other?

How would you describe my products or service?

1. Satisfied? 2. Happy? Other?

How would you describe the overall experience?

1. Satisfied? 2. Happy? Other?

In terms of a grade, satisfied is a C and Happy is an A. Aim for Happy!

Ask them to give examples of how you could get better.

What exactly would make them HAPPY as your customer?

Ask them for ideas to find new customers.

Ask yourself, how do my competitors sell it?

Find unique differences "in your favor" and promote them.

If you have difficulties with this, ask your "promoters" for some ideas?

Describe who your worst customer is. Discuss why. This will provide valuable insights.

TARGET QUALIFYING SYSTEM

☐ The logo looks good on a HATCLP and the artwork is easy to convert. The simpler the better. This is "THE QUALIFIER"! #1. Move on, there are millions of targets.

☐ This customer's base or segment of it are predominant hat wearers.

☐ We have a referral.

☐ The probability of purchasing 1000+ units is high.

☐ The probability of purchasing 100+ units is high and the opportunity for multiple uses of the HATCLPS is likely. For example, events, special occasions, milestones & holidays.

☐ The entity has similar marketing products or services like us and could be a strategic partner. For example, an embroidery company that markets hats and clothing to businesses for promotional activities.

☐ The opportunity is part of a phenomenon, a niche industry or a new category of business with the potential for high profits. For example, the Mary Jane industry has been an explosive business avenue recently. Examples of phenomenons are TRUMP, MAGA, BLM, ANTIFA, FJB, LET'S GO BRANDON. Phenomenons can be industry specific as well.

☐ If the target does not meet the #1 qualifier it has to meet both of the following requirements in-order for us to move forward.
1. The target at a minimum should meet three of the other qualifiers.
2. Target deemed as viable after analysis and approved by the president.

Okay, so, how do you build a qualifying tool? Think about it this way you have the chance to craft a set of criteria or questions that will help you filter out those who are not a good fit and focus on those who are most likely to be interested in what you have to offer.
Identify the ideal customer circumstances that make them the perfect fit. This means understanding what the customer values and what they are looking for in a business and aligning that with the unique value and services you provide.

☐

You get to choose who your ideal customers are. This means that you have the power to create a vision for the kind of customers you want to attract.

☐

Are you a retailer, wholesaler, B2B or service provider? You set the parameters here.

☐

Does the prospect have reasonable purchase power and potential multiple income pathways for you to tap into?

☐

Is the prospect a business and have a similar target market?

☐

Does the entity have comparable products or service like us and would compliment our business. They could be a strategic partner in the form of referring one another.

☐ The entity has the same target market as us and could be a strategic partner because they offer a different product or service to that market.

In summary, creating a qualifying tool is an effective way to use your time and resources wisely by focusing on the most promising prospects. It involves developing a list of qualifying criteria in the from of questions and determining how to use the answers to those questions to draw a clear conclusion about whether a prospect is an ideal customer. This process will help you to make the most of your time and resources by focusing on those customers who are most likely to benefit from doing business with you.

Referrals are a game changer!

Promoters are your biggest fans and generally spend the most money. They also love what you do and talk you up to others. They usually account for 10 - 20% of a company's customer base. List 3 of your customers you consider promoters.

How do you engage with this group in your business?

1.

2.

3.

Buyers are customers that like what you offer and buy what you're selling but that's usually it. They account for about 50 - 70% of the customer base. What needs to be done to make these customers promoters?

How do you engage with this group in your business?

List 3 of your customers you consider buyers.

1.

2.

3.

Demoters are the customers that come around and may or may not buy. Generally, they are there for a free bee, a handout and have an affinity for always finding something bad about your business. They have no merit for things they say and usually spread invalid information to others about you. List 3 demoters. Drop these people like a bad habit. They are usually about 10% of a business's customer base.

1.

2.

3.

At HATCLPS, we understand the importance of regularly evaluating and redefining your target audience. That is why we are partnering with ACE Marketing to assist our customers with evaluations and building customized practical marketing tools. Our goal is to help you understand and reach your target audience in the most effective way possible.

Building a qualifying tool is essential and crucial to effectively reach your target market and engage your audience. In the earlier pages, we discussed the importance of identifying and understanding your target market and audience, as well as identifying niche areas to help establish a path to effectively reach your customers. By doing this, you will be able to think about who your customers are and what value you provide them within your business. This understanding is crucial in building a qualifying tool that will help you effectively reach and engage with your target market and audience.

Communicating the value that your customers experience by doing business with you is essential to building trust and fostering strong relationships with them. This is known as your "value message", which highlights the benefits that your customers receive when they choose your company over others.

However, not all companies are effective in communicating this value to their customers. In fact, according to a survey of executives, only 15% of sales calls effectively communicate the value that a company can offer to its customers.

To ensure that your company's value message is being effectively communicated, it's important to define it clearly. This means identifying the unique benefits that your customers experience when they do business with you and making sure that these benefits are clearly communicated through all your marketing and sales efforts. By doing this, you will be able to communicate the value that your customers receive when they choose your company and differentiate yourself from your competition.

Word of Mouth Strategy (WOM), peer to peer!

Don't waste another minute get started and list your 20 top customers based on revenue and their love for your products and or services. By understanding who your best customers are, you can tailor your marketing efforts and business strategies to attract more customers who share the same likes and values. This means that not only will you retain your most profitable buyers, but you will also be on your way to gaining more people who are likely to be just as loyal and valuable. By taking the time to perform and complete this exercise, you will gain valuable insights into your existing customer base and be able to create more targeted and effective marketing campaigns, leading to increased revenue and growth for your business.

Below, LIST YOUR BEST CUSTOMERS to initiate the HATCLP peer to peer marketing system. You provide them with 2 – 3 HATCLPS, one for them and the others to hand out.

1.
2.
3.
4.
5.
6.
7.
8.
9.
10.
11.
12.
13.
14.
15.
16.
17.
18.
19.
20.

Summary

Word-of-mouth marketing is an incredibly powerful tool for any business and there is no better source for this than your absolute best customers. When your top customers talk up your business to their friends and family, they are acting as brand ambassadors for you. This means that their recommendations are highly valued and trusted by those in their personal network. By leveraging these relationships, you can attract new candidates who are likely to share similar interests and values as your best customers. These referrals are more likely to convert into paying regulars and be loyal to your business, leading to increased revenue and profitability. In short, having your best patrons talk up your business to their friends and family is a highly effective way to tap into new customer pools, making you more money in the long run.

Compliments on *prioritizing customer engagement* and word-of-mouth marketing as a key strategy for your business. You are on the fast track to success and are more likely to acquire higher quality leads from your customer base. It's clear that word-of-mouth marketing is the most applicable way to gain new customers, with most of all business coming from referrals. By utilizing our system, you will have practical strategies and support to help you connect with customers in a powerful way and enhance your overall customer engagement. With less than 1% of businesses having a strategy for this approach, you are already standing out from the competition and are on your way to driving actual results to the outcomes you desire.

Are you ready to take your business to the next level? It's time to tap into the power of your best customers - *your promoters*, your fan club. They are the ones who have already talked you up and are the foundation of your word-of-mouth marketing system. And now, we are giving you a powerful tool to supercharge their impact: **THE HATCLP**. By distributing these to *your promoters*, you will be giving them a tangible way to share their love for your brand with others. This will generate powerful stories about how they became your biggest fans and will help you acquire an entirely new set of buyers who share the same wants, needs, likes, behaviors, and buying habits. Do not wait - now is the time to act and put this marketing weapon into use for your business. Congratulations on making this groundbreaking decision, now let's get started on the road to success!

Scan below to visit HATCLPS.COM

www.ingramcontent.com/pod-product-compliance
Lightning Source LLC
Chambersburg PA
CBHW072019230526
45479CB00008B/305